# Things to spot

Can you spot one of these Christmas decorations on each double page?

chocolate bell

toy Santa

crib

Christmas cracker

stocking

reindeer

lantern

mistletoe

star

candy stick

bauble

garland

gingerbread house

### Christmas presents

There is a little wrapped Christmas present to spot on every double page.

### Gingerbread men

There is one jolly gingerbread man to find on every double page.

# Surf's up!

One morning, just before Christmas, Kira was surfing in the ocean near her house. Riding the crest of a giant wave, Kira had a great view of the beach, and all her friends. There was Emma, building a sandcastle, and Ben, licking a strawberry ice cream. Maria and Carlos were doing handstands. Even her puppy, Max, was digging in the sand. Then, as the wave crashed over her, Kira caught a glimpse of something that looked very out of place on the busy beach.

**Can you spot Kira's friends? What else has Kira seen?**

# Puzzle Christmas

Susannah Leigh

Illustrated by Brenda Haw

## Contents

Edited by Jenny Tyler and Catriona Clarke
Design co-ordinator: Laura Parker
Additional design: Vicky Arrowsmith

# About this book

This book is about a girl called Kira and her magical Christmas adventure. There are puzzles to solve on every double page. If you get stuck, the answers are on pages 31 and 32. Kira loves everything about Christmas – especially the presents! But she has never seen snow, because where she lives it is always hot and sunny. So this year she has written a letter to Santa.

This is Kira. →

This is Kira's puppy, Max. →

Tropical Island
Puzzle World
December

Dear Santa,
I hope you are well. For Christmas, I would like it to snow – enough for a snowball fight please. Where I live it is always hot and sunny. Give my love to all the reindeer.

Kira x

Santa
stmas Land
World

ICES

# Rio's story

Hardly daring to believe her eyes, Kira rode a wave back to the beach. She raced through the palm trees and, sure enough, there stood a little reindeer, looking lost and frightened.

"What are you doing here?" Kira asked kindly. "Can I help you?"

She hadn't really expected the reindeer to answer, but when he did, Kira found she wasn't surprised. She knew magical things could happen at Christmas time. But the reindeer's story was rather muddled and Kira had trouble making sense of it.

**Can you put the reindeer's story in the right order?**

...now I have lost my magic bell. Without it, I can't fly back home to Christmas Land, and Santa promised –

...from a boy called Lucas, who has never seen the sea.

Hello, my name is Rio. I'm Santa's littlest reindeer.

Now, Lucas wanted a seashell for Christmas. Santa wondered if he'd have time to find one, so I thought I would surprise Santa by...

This year Santa got a letter...

...flying over here and getting one. But...

– that I could pull the sleigh on Christmas Eve. Oh dear!

# Hitching a lift

When Kira heard Rio's story, she was worried. "Christmas Eve is tomorrow," she said. "We have to get you back to Christmas Land so you can pull Santa's sleigh."

Rio shook his head sadly. "I can't find my bell anywhere."

"It will be OK, Rio. I'll help you look for it," said Kira.

They walked along the beach searching for the bell, but they couldn't find it.

"This is hopeless," Kira said. "We'll have to think of some other way to get you home." They had come to the port, busy with boats of all shapes and sizes. Suddenly, Kira had an idea.

"These boats go all over the world," she said. "One of them might be heading your way, Rio!"

**Is there a boat that Rio could hitch a lift with?**

# Chilly voyage

Kira helped Rio aboard the boat, but it set sail before she could jump off again.

"Oh no! Rio, what am I going to do?" she gasped.

"Don't worry," Rio said. "When you get back, it will seem like you've been away no time at all. Santa's Christmas magic will see to that. Now, we'd better hide in these barrels so nobody finds us."

After a choppy voyage, the boat stopped. The barrels were loaded onto a plane...

...then a train, which rattled through the night, before stopping at the edge of an icy world.

Brr. I'm cold!

Take my blanket.

Christmas Land! Hop on my back, Kira and I'll carry you across the ice.

CHRISTMAS LAND

Can you find a safe way across the ice to
Christmas Land? Make sure you avoid the cracks.

11

# Light show

Rio and Kira scrambled ashore. In the distance they saw swirly lights, dancing across the morning sky.

Rio kicked his hooves in delight. "Those are the magic lights of Christmas Land, and it's not far from here to Santa's house. We're nearly there!"

They wandered among tall pillars of ice in the frosty glow. Then, out of the corner of her eye, Kira saw one of the pillars move. She looked closer and suddenly realized that they were surrounded by lots of polar bears!

**How many polar bears can you spot?**

# Polar slide

The polar bears came closer and closer. Kira was afraid, until one of them shouted, "Hello, Rio!"

The bears were pleased to see Rio, and eager to hear his story. "Lost your magic bell, eh?" said the biggest bear. "That's bad news. Never mind, Rio. We'll take you to Snowman Village – it's not far from there to Santa's. Hop onto our backs and hang on tight. It's going to be a slippery ride avoiding all the fallen trees and snoozing seals."

**Can you find a way down the icy maze to the village below? Watch out for the fallen trees and sleepy seals.**

SNOWMAN VILLAGE

# Snow ho ho

With a whizz and a whoosh, they slipped to the end of the slide. "That was fun!" cried Kira.

"We'd better leave you here," whispered the bears. "The snow people are a bit nervous of us."

Now Kira stared in amazement at the sight before her. There were snow men and snow women, snow babies and snow pets. And what's more, there were piles and piles of snow!

"My Christmas wish," she cried. "Enough snow for a—"

"Snowball fight." Rio finished.

Rio introduced Kira to the snow people, and everyone got ready to play.

**How many are on Kira's team and how many on Rio's?**

Let's play!

Find your teams... and plenty of snowballs!

16

# Forest trail

After the fight, Kira collapsed, breathless. "Who won?" she laughed.

"I've no idea!" Rio giggled. "But wasn't it fun?"

"Great fun! Oh, but Rio, it's getting late and starting to snow. Let's get you back to Santa."

"OK," Rio said. "Come on. Santa lives on the other side of Frosty Forest."

They walked through a forest of frosty pines and snowy glades...

...until they came to a cosy-looking house.

Rio and Kira peeped inside.

Rio gasped at what he heard. "Do you know who that
is, Kira? And do you remember what he asked for?
I completely forgot!"

"I remember," Kira said. "And I think I have something
that might help."

**Who is the boy and how can Kira help?**

# Tree trouble

"Lucas can have my seashell."

Rio took the seashell. "Thank you, Kira. Santa can take it with him tonight."

"It's getting dark already!" Kira said. "Are we nearly there yet?"

"Just around this corner – oh..."

Around the corner was a beautiful sight. Decorated Christmas trees sparkled in the forest. But the littlest tree was dull and bare, and beside it stood an old elf, muttering to himself.

"Oh dear, oh dear. I've lost the decorations for this little tree."

"We can help," Kira said kindly. "What have you lost?"

"It's quite a list I'm afraid: five red apples, two blue baubles, a gold star, one white bauble, four popcorn strings, three green baubles and an angel doll."

**Can you find the missing things?**

# Toy maze

As Kira placed the star on top of the little tree, it magically became bright with lights.

"Thank you, thank you!" the old elf called, as Kira and Rio waved goodbye.

At the edge of the forest there was a little red train waiting for them.

"We're nearly there," Rio cried. "We just need to hop on this train. Do you think you can drive it to that red door over there, Kira?"

"I think so, but we'd better watch out for those giant toys."

**Can you find the way along the track to the little red door?**

# Meet the family

They hopped off the train, and Rio turned to Kira. "I'll take you to meet my family before we go to see Santa. I do hope he's not cross with me."

Rio and Kira stepped into a cosy stable. "Rio! Where have you been?" called one of the reindeer.

"Hi Dad, I went to Tropical Island but I lost my magic bell," Rio said.

Rudy

Rex

Rose

Rolf

"Oh, Rio. We were so worried about you!"

"I'm sorry," Rio said. "This is Kira. She helped me get home."

"And I think I can guess your names," Kira smiled.

**Can you tell which reindeer is which?**

# Wonderful workshop

The reindeer laughed. "Clever, Kira. Do you want to meet Santa now?" Kira nodded excitedly, and Rio led her to Santa's workshop. Elves were busy making toys and singing Christmas songs. Then...

"Ho ho ho!" boomed a jolly voice.

"Santa, it's really you!" Kira cried.

But Rio wasn't so sure about seeing Santa. "I'm sorry I flew off without telling you," he whispered. "And lost my magic bell."

CYCLE BELL

TREE BELL

JINGLE BELL

FAIRY BELL

CHRISTMAS BELL

REINDEER BELL (MAGIC)

"I know you were only trying to help, Rio," said Santa kindly. "Now, let's find you another magic bell for tonight."

"You mean...?" Rio began.

"Yes," Santa said. "You're just in time to lead my sleigh. Kira can come too. Now, there are lots of bells here, but only one is magical."

Can you find the magic bell? Look at the posters to give you a clue.

# Christmas Eve!

Later, on the most magical night of the year, Rio proudly pulled Santa's sleigh through the starry sky.

Kira looked down with delight from her seat next to Santa. "I can see the whole world from up here!" she cried. "Look, there are the snow people – and the polar bears. The little old elf and his Christmas trees are down there, too. There's the train track, and that's Lucas's house. Don't forget to give him his shell, Santa!"

**Can you spot everything?**

# Magical morning

Rio had been right. When Santa finally dropped Kira back home, no time had passed and everyone was still on the beach as before. Kira began to wonder if she had imagined her magical adventure.

But when Kira woke up on Christmas morning and spotted a special present at the end of her bed, she knew she hadn't imagined it after all. Her puppy, Max, had a surprise for her, too.

**Can you see the special present? Who is it from? What has Max found and where did he find it? (You may to need to look back through the book.)**

Kira

love from

30

# Answers

## Pages 4-5

Kira's friends are circled here. Kira has also spotted a reindeer hiding in the trees.

## Pages 6-7

1. Hello my name is Rio, I'm Santa's littlest reindeer.
2. This year Santa got a letter...
3. ...from a boy called Lucas, who has never seen the sea.
4. Now, Lucas wanted a seashell for Christmas. Santa wondered if he'd have time to find one, so I thought I would surprise Santa by...
5. ...flying over here and getting one. But...
6. ...now I have lost my magic bell. Without it, I can't fly back home to Christmas Land, and Santa promised –
7. – that I could pull the sleigh on Christmas Eve. Oh dear!

## Pages 8-9

This boat has just delivered trees from Christmas Land, and is about to sail back there.

## Pages 10-11

## Pages 12-13

There are 12 bears hiding in the ice.

## Pages 14-15

## Pages 16-17

There are four snow people on Kira's team and four on Rio's team.

## Pages 18-19

The boy in the house is Lucas, who wrote to Santa asking for a seashell. Rio can take Kira's shell to give to Lucas.

## Pages 20-21

The missing decorations are circled here.

## Pages 22-23

The train must follow the tracks this way to get to the other side.

## Pages 24-25

**Rolf** is the reindeer with the blue nose.

**Rose** has a ring in her nose.

**Rex** has a light brown tail.

**Rudy** has a red nose.

**Rita** is the reindeer with a bow on her tail.

**Roger** has pale tips on his tail fur.

## Pages 26-27

Rio's magical reindeer bell is on the table with the food.

## Pages 28-29

All the places in Christmas Land that Kira and Rio have visited are circled here.

# Did you spot everything?

Did you find a gingerbread man on every double page?

And did you find the Christmas presents?

## Page 30

The special present is a snowball from her friend Rio.

Max has found Rio's lost reindeer bell. He found it near the beach.

This list shows where the Christmas decorations are hidden.

| pages | objects |
|---|---|
| 4 | bauble |
| 7 | mistletoe |
| 9 | lantern |
| 11 | candy stick |
| 12 | Christmas cracker |
| 14 | gingerbread house |
| 16 | star |
| 19 | toy Santa |
| 20 | crib |
| 23 | stocking |
| 25 | reindeer |
| 26 | chocolate bell |
| 29 | garland |

First published in 2008, by Usborne Publishing Ltd, Usborne House, 83-85 Saffron Hill, London, EC1N 8RT.
www.usborne.com
Copyright © 2008 Usborne Publishing Ltd. The name Usborne and the devices ⚓ ⊕ are Trademarks of Usborne Publishing Ltd. All rights reserved. No part of this publication may be reproduced, stored in a retrieval system or transmitted in any form or by any means, electronic, mechanical, photocopying, recording, or otherwise, without previous permission of the publisher.

Printed in China.